Just Desserts

The Way To A Vegan's Sweet Tooth

By Heena Modi

Just Desserts: The Way To A Vegan's Sweet Tooth by Heena Modi.
Published by Heena Modi.
www.PlantShift.com

Copyright © 2021 Heena Modi.

Photographers
Willy Wong, Heena Modi and Arjun Shah.

Designer
Urvee Rupani.

Printed and bound by
The Print Shop,
4 Pinner Green,
Pinner,
Middlesex.
HA5 2AA .
www.printshoppinner.co.uk

Printed in UK

ISBN 978-1-80049-904-1

No part of this book may be reprinted or distributed without the written permission of the author. Digital reproduction or redistribution is also prohibited.

Introduction

I've been vegan since early 2008 and I've never looked back! I feel fab. Physically great, emotionally aligned and ethically, at peace.

What was a diet, soon became a lifestyle, and I can't imagine living any other way!

I want to help others achieve the same.

Food, especially desserts, shouldn't be a barrier to going vegan or staying vegan. I want to show everyone how easy it is to make delicious plant-based desserts and know that going vegan doesn't mean missing out!

 @PlantShift    @PlantShift    @PlantShift

What's Inside...

For The Cookie Monsters 2

    Linzer Cookies 3

    Thumbprint Cookies 5

    Peanut Butter Cookies 7

    Oat Cookies 9

Eastern Delights 12

    Penda 13

    Dudhi No Halwo 15

    Halwa 17

    Pista Burfi 19

    Shrikhand 21

Nuts About Truffles 24

    Coffee Truffles 25

    Extra Chocolatey Truffles 27

    Pistachio Coated Truffles 29

    Flakey Truffles 31

    Bounty Truffles 33

    Salted Caramel Peanut Butter Truffles 35

All Things Chocolate 38

    Chocolate Brownie With A Twist 39

    Red Velvet Chocolate Chip Cupcakes 41

    Chocolatey Cupcakes 43

    Chocolate Coated Peanut Surprise 45

    Choc And Nut Delight..47

    Chocolatey Cupcakes With A Surprise....................49

Cheesecake Cheesecake And More Cheesecake................**52**

    Gingerbread Cheesecake.....................................53

    Strawberry Cheesecake.......................................55

    Mini Chocolate Cheesecakes................................57

    The Beauty Of Biscoff...59

Family Creations..**62**

    Sweet And Savoury Delight.................................63

    Weetabix Paak...65

Gifts From Europe..**68**

    Tiramisu..69

    Meringue..71

In Ten Minutes Or Less..**74**

    QCC [Quick Crispy & Cooling]..............................75

    Cocoaban Delight..77

Recipes That Need Time To Chill Or Set.....................**80**

    Chia Delight..81

    Peanut Butter Cookies...7

    Halwa..17

    Gingerbread Cheesecake....................................53

    Strawberry Cheesecake......................................55

    Mini Chocolate Cheesecakes...............................57

    The Beauty Of Biscoff..59

About The Author...**83**

Other Books By Heena Modi....................................**85**

Gratitude

I could not have created this book without Willy. I'm deeply grateful for his love of making food, arranging it beautifully and then capturing it on camera. He's also a bit techy so he knew about all sorts of things to do with files types, how to make the quality of the photos optimum and so on.

I can't thank Ash enough. His eagle eyes were exactly what I needed when I was working on ensuring that the recipes were consistent, made sense and easy to follow.

Finally, Urvee. Her creativity, openness, objectivity and desire to understand and deliver what I wanted was jaw-dropping! Also, when I wasn't sure about something, she'd create a variety of designs, which helped us both better understand what brought about a thumbs up and what didn't.

Last but not least, there are a number of people who have supported me, before and since, Plant Shift was created. There are far too many to mention but I'll have a go.

A Few Things To Keep In Mind

Ingredients

Coconut Milk
When I refer to using a can of coconut milk, this is the preparation that needs to be done beforehand.

- At least 1 day earlier, place a can of coconut milk in the fridge
- Put it upside down
- When you're making the recipe, remove the can of coconut milk from the fridge, turn it the right way up and open it
- Carefully scoop out the cream, which should have separated from the coconut water and solidified
- I keep a few cans in the fridge so that I always have one to hand
- I'm hot on reducing waste, so when you've finished making your delightful dessert, do a quick internet search for 'recipes using coconut water' and that will give you lots of ideas about how to utilise it, rather than, throwing it away

Soft cheese
When I refer to using soft vegan cheese, my preference is Tesco and Asda's own.

Icing sugar
Some brands add dried egg white to their icing sugar, which encourages me to buy one that is labelled as vegan. I usually opt for Sainsbury's own.

Measurements
All the measurements are based on UK standards.
I've used measuring cups and measuring teaspoons and tablespoons, rather than, regular utensils that are found in the home.
If you're in a different country please check whether the measuring tools I've used align with yours as this will affect the outcome of the recipe.
If your measuring equipment is different or you'd prefer to, for example, measure in pounds instead of grams, then a converter like this should help https://www.omnicalculator.com/food/grams-to-cups.

" Eating a vegan diet could be the "single biggest way" to reduce your environmental impact on earth, a new study suggests.

Researchers at the University of Oxford found that cutting meat and dairy products from your diet could reduce an individual's carbon footprint from food by up to 73 per cent. "

Source - The Independent

For The Cookie Monsters

Linzer Cookies

Thumbprint Cookies

Peanut Butter Cookies

Oat Cookies

Linzer Cookies

Serves: 10 | Total Time: 1 hour

Ingredients

- ⅔ cup of finely ground almonds
- ⅓ cup of coconut flour
- ¼ teaspoon of bicarbonate of soda
- ¼ teaspoon of Himalayan rock salt
- ⅓ cup of coconut oil (at room temperature)
- ¼ cup of Golden Syrup
- 1 tablespoon of pure vanilla extract
- 1 jar of raspberry jam (you won't need all of it)

Method

1. Sift the **ground almonds, coconut flour, bicarbonate of soda** and **salt** into a large bowl and set aside
2. In a smaller bowl, use a hand blender to mix the **coconut oil, Golden Syrup** and **vanilla extract** until it has combined
3. Use a blender to combine the wet ingredients and dry ingredients
4. Put the dough in the middle of a large piece of greaseproof paper, cover it with another sheet of the same and use a rolling pin to make the dough about 4 mm thick
5. Put it in the freezer for 30 minutes and preheat the oven to 180 Celsius
6. Line a baking tray with greaseproof paper
7. Remove the dough from the freezer and use a cookie cutter to create the cookies
8. Use a smaller cookie cutter to create a hole in the middle of half of the cookies
9. Take the cutouts from the holes and add them to the dough to re-use them
10. The dough gets sticky very quickly so you may only be able to make about 4 at a time
11. When the dough gets sticky, put it back in the middle of the greaseproof paper, put the other sheet on top, roll it again and put it in the freezer for about 3 minutes
12. When the oven is ready and you have an equal number of cookies that are with and without holes, bake them until the edges are lightly golden. This will take between 3 and 5 minutes
13. Leave them on the baking tray for 2 minutes before moving them or they will break
14. When they have completely cooled, put 1 teaspoon of **jam** on each of the 'whole' cookies and then add a cookie with the hole in it and press them together lightly

Tip: If you don't have a smaller cookie cutter, you can use a knife to make the holes in the cookies.

Storage: If you can resist, and if kept in an airtight container, the cookies will last for about three days. They start softening after that.

Allergens: Nuts

Thumbprint Cookies

Serves: 16 | Total Time: 35 minutes

Ingredients

1 cup of ground almonds	1 teaspoon of ground cinnamon
1 cup of brown rice flour	½ cup of coconut oil
1 ½ cups of raw whole almonds	½ cup of maple syrup
½ teaspoon of salt	1 jar of jam (you won't need all of it)

Method

1. Preheat the oven to 180 degrees
2. Use a pestle and mortar to crush the **almonds**
3. Apart from the **jam**, combine all the ingredients in a large bowl
4. Line a baking tray with greaseproof paper
5. Use a tablespoon to remove some dough. Roll it in your hands to create a ball and keep going until you have no dough left
6. Space them evenly on a baking tray leaving about 2 cm between them
7. Use your thumb to make an indentation into the middle of each cookie
8. Bake until the cookies are evenly browned, which will take 15 - 20 minutes
9. Remove the cookies from the oven and set them aside to cool for 20 minutes
10. Use a teaspoon to add some **jam** to each cookie or add it just before you're ready to eat them

Tip: If you are going to add the jam just before eating the cookie, keeping them in an airtight container is fine. If you want to have them ready with the jam on them, keep the container in the fridge.

Allergens: Nuts

Peanut Butter Cookies

Serves: 16 | Total Time: 2 hours 35 minutes

Ingredients

¾ cup of unrefined brown sugar

2 tablespoons of maple syrup

½ cup of smooth peanut butter

¼ cup of sunflower oil or any other oil that doesn't have a strong flavour

¼ cup of softened vegan buttery spread

⅓ cup of smooth apple sauce

1¼ cups of flour blend - I used one that contained four different types of flour

¾ teaspoon of bicarbonate of soda

½ teaspoon of baking powder

¼ teaspoon of salt

1 tablespoon of sugar

Method

1. Mix the **sugar, peanut butter, apple sauce, oil** and **maple syrup** in a large bowl

2. Add all the other ingredients and stir

3. Cover it with cling film and put it in the refrigerator for about 2 hours or until it's firm

4. Heat the oven to 190 Celsius and line a baking tray with greaseproof paper

5. Shape the dough into balls and put them on the lined baking tray

6. They expand so keep them about 6 cm apart

7. Use a fork dipped in **sugar** to flatten each cookie and create a criss-cross pattern on each one

8. Bake for about 10 minutes or until they become a light golden brown

9. Remove them from the oven but leave them on the tray for 10 minutes and then put them onto a wire rack so they can cool. They will break if you move them too early.

Storage: If you can resist, and if kept in an airtight container, they will be good for three days.

Allergens: Peanuts  **and Gluten**

Oat Cookies

Serves: 12 | Total Time: 45 minutes

Ingredients

1 ¾ cups of pecan halves	½ a cup of maple syrup
2 cups of oats (divided)	3.5 tablespoons of liquid coconut oil
¾ cup of plain flour	2 tablespoons of almond milk
½ cup of brown sugar	2 teaspoons of vanilla extract
1 teaspoon of bicarbonate of soda	⅓ cup of diced pitted dates (heaped)
½ teaspoon of cinnamon powder	½ teaspoon of flour
½ teaspoon of fine grain sea salt	¼ cup of mini dark chocolate chips

Method

1. Preheat the oven to 160 Celsius
2. Put a sheet of greaseproof paper on a large baking tray
3. Toast the **pecan nuts** for about 9 minutes until they are golden and fragrant
4. Remove the **pecan nuts** from the oven and set them aside for a few minutes
5. Increase the oven temperature to 175 Celsius
6. Put the **pecan nuts** and 1 cup of **oats** in a food processor. Stop processing when they are roughly chopped - over-processing it will release the oils in the nuts
7. In a large bowl, mix the contents of the food processor with the remaining cup of **oats, flour, sugar, bicarbonate of soda, cinnamon,** and **salt**
8. In a separate bowl, mix the **maple syrup, coconut oil, milk** and **vanilla**
9. Pour the wet mixture onto the dry ingredients and mix it until it has combined. If the dough is sticky, all is well
10. Chop the **dates**, so that they're about the size of a raisin, put them in a small bowl, add ½ a teaspoon of **flour** and toss them until the dates are coated - this will stop them from sticking together
11. Take enough dough for 1 cookie and roll it into a ball
12. Put it on the greaseproof paper and use the palm of your hand to flatten it
13. If the dough sticks to your hands, use a little water to wet your hands and continue
14. Leave about 5 cm between each cookie
15. Bake them until they are golden brown underneath. This will take about 10 minutes
16. Take them out of the oven and leave them on the greaseproof paper for about 3 minutes
17. Put the cookies onto a cooling rack for 15 minutes

Storage: If you can resist, they will last longer in an airtight container.

Allergens: Nuts and Gluten

> You may be asked what you're doing
> They may challenge your motivations
> It might hurt when you feel mocked
> But will you have peace of mind if you're not true to yourself?

Source - Heena Modi

Eastern Delights

Penda

Dudhi No Halwa

Halwa

Pista Burfi

Shrikhand

Ingredients

- 1 cup of ground almonds
- 4 tablespoons of coconut flour
- 8 tablespoons of soft brown sugar
- 3 generous pinches of fine sea salt
- ½ teaspoon of finely ground cardamom powder
- ¼ teaspoon of saffron strands
- 4 teaspoons of soya milk or other non-dairy milk
- 4 tablespoons of sweet syrup - I used Bali Nutra Coconut Syrup
- ¼ cup of soya milk or other non-dairy milk
- ¼ cup of sliced almonds

Method

1. Heat 4 teaspoons of **soya milk**
2. Put the **saffron** in the milk, turn the heat off and let sit for 5 minutes
3. In a bowl, mix the **ground almonds, coconut flour, sugar, salt** and **cardamom**
4. Add the **syrup** and soya milk (which has saffron in it) to the bowl and mix it well
5. Add the ¼ cup of **soya milk** and mix
6. If the dough is soft, all is well
7. Line a baking tray with greaseproof paper
8. Put a small amount of dough on the greaseproof paper and use your hands or a biscuit cutter to mould it into discs
9. Garnish each 1 with **chopped almonds**
10. Bake at 150 Celsius for 9-10 minutes (they will expand a little)
11. Let them cool completely before serving

Storage: Keep them in the fridge, in an airtight container and they should keep for a week.

Allergens: Nuts
The milk may contain one or more of the major allergens.

Ingredients

2 handfuls of almonds (divided)

1 medium sized Dudhi also known as bottle gourd vegetable - roughly 30 cm long with the widest part being about 6 cm in diameter

2 tablespoons of olive oil

1 teaspoon of cardamom

1 splash of vegan green food colouring

Sugar - see step 7

Method

1. Slice the **almonds** and set them aside
2. Wash, peel and grate the **Dudhi**
3. Squeeze the **Dudhi**, to remove as much of the juice as possible
4. Weigh what's left of the **Dudhi** and make a note of the weight
5. Pour the **olive oil** into a non-stick pan, heat and add the **Dudhi**
6. Using a medium heat, stir the **Dudhi** for 5 minutes (this will remove some of the excess juice and make it softer)
7. Using the measurement that you noted down in step 4, work out ¾ of that amount and this will tell you how much **sugar** is needed
8. Put the **sugar** into the pan with the **Dudhi** and stir
9. Increase the heat and keep stirring
10. After all the **sugar** has melted, reduce the heat and keep stirring
11. Set aside a handful of **almonds** for step 16 and finely chop the rest for the next step
12. Add the **green colouring, cardamom** and finely chopped **almonds** and keep stirring
13. Stop stirring when the mixture turns into a ball that is easily detached from the pan
14. Use a spoon to take some of the mixture and roll it into a round disk
15. Repeat until you have used all of the mixture
16. Slice the remaining almonds and use them to garnish the pieces before putting them in the fridge

Alternative method:
Instead of the final two steps, you could put the mixture in a tray, flatten it, garnish it with the almonds and then cut it into square pieces once it's cooled.

Storage: If you put them in an airtight container and store it in the fridge, they should keep for a week.

Allergens: Nuts

Halwa

Serves: 24 | Total Time: 3 hours

Ingredients

- 100g of cornflour
- 1 litre of water
- 600g of brown vegan sugar
- ⅛ teaspoon of vegan food colouring (your choice of colour)
- 1 handful of blanched and flaked almonds
- 1 handful of whole pistachios
- 4 tablespoons of sunflower oil (divided)
- 3 tablespoons of vegan margarine (divided)
- A small amount of vegan margarine to grease your dish
- 2 teaspoons of ground cardamom
- 2 tablespoons of desiccated coconut (optional)

Method

1. In a large non-stick pan, using a high temperature, mix the **cornflour** with the **water**
2. Once combined, add the **sugar** and stir continuously until the mixture is boiling
3. Lower the temperature to a medium heat and continue stirring (you may notice some 'lumps' of sugar but keep stirring until the mixture is thick and fully combined)
4. Add the **food colouring**
5. Stir until the **colour** is evenly distributed
6. Use a pestle and mortar to crush the **almonds** and **pistachios**, add them to the pan and continue stirring for about 5 minutes, ensuring that the mixture is not sticking to the bottom or the sides of the pan
7. Reduce the heat to a low setting and add 1 tablespoon of **oil** and stir for 1-2 minutes until it's combined
8. Add 1 tablespoon of the **margarine** and stir for 1-2 minutes until combined
9. Keep repeating steps 7 and 8 until you've used all the **oil** and **margarine**
10. When the mixture falls off the spoon but isn't runny like syrup, you know it's ready
11. Now add the **cardamom** and mix for 1-2 minutes
12. Turn the heat off
13. Use the small amount of **margarine** to grease the bottom and sides of a rectangular dish and pour the mixture into it
14. When all of the mixture is in the dish, give it a gentle shake to remove any air bubbles and ensure even distribution
15. Sprinkle the **desiccated coconut** over the mixture
16. Let the Halwa set at room temperature and then transfer it to the fridge
17. Cut it into pieces when it is firm

Storage: If you put the Halwa in an airtight container and store it in the fridge, it should keep for three days.

Allergens: Nuts

Ingredients

- 100g of creamed coconut
- 150g of coarsely ground pistachios
- 50g of golden syrup
- ¼ teaspoon of vanilla essence
- ½ teaspoon of cardamom powder
- 1 cup of flaked almonds, whole pistachios or pieces of dried fruit

Method

1. Use cling film to line a takeaway container (roughly 17 cm x 11 cm)
2. Remove the **pistachios** from their shells and use a food processor, spice grinder or blender to grind them
3. Melt the **creamed coconut** by putting it in a bowl, whilst it's in the plastic packaging and putting the bowl in a pan of hot water
4. Blend the **ground pistachios, golden syrup, vanilla essence** and **cardamom powder** together
5. Once the **creamed coconut** has softened, add it to the blender and quickly blend all the ingredients together (if you aren't quick, it will solidify)
6. Pour the mixture into the container mentioned in step 1
7. Decorate the mixture with **flaked almonds, whole pistachios** or **pieces of dried fruit**
8. Leave it to cool for 15 minutes and then put it in the fridge for 30 minutes
9. Remove the container from the fridge, pull the cling film out of it, take the Burfi off the cling film and then cut it to size

Storage: If you put the Burfi in an airtight container and store it in the fridge, it should keep for a week.

Allergens: Nuts

Shrikhand
Serves: 6 | Total Time: 40 minutes

Ingredients

400g of Alpro Greek Style Plain Yoghurt
1 tablespoon of vegan icing sugar
¾ teaspoon of finely ground cardamom
1 tablespoon of sliced almonds

1 tablespoon of coarsely ground pistachio
5 strands of saffron

Method

1. Put the **yoghurt** in a container that's deep enough for you to easily mix the ingredients in
2. Use a spoon to make a gap in the **yoghurt**
3. Put the **cardamom** and **icing sugar** in the gap
4. Fold the **yoghurt** over and mix carefully
5. Have a taste and decide if it needs more **sugar** or **cardamom**
6. Slice the **almonds** and coarsely grind the **pistachios**
7. Add most of the **pistachios** and all of the **saffron** and mix again
8. Put the Shrikhand in something that you'd like to serve it in
9. Use the rest of the **pistachio** and all of the **almonds** to garnish it
10. Put it in the fridge for 30 minutes (or more) before consuming (this is optional but I find it tastes better after it's been left to marinate and has cooled in the fridge)

Variation
You can flavour it with vanilla or pieces of fruit.

Storage: Without fruit, it will keep in the fridge for at least three days.
Timing: If you prepare the almonds and pistachios in advance, making the Shrikhand will take less than ten minutes.

Allergens: Nuts and **Soya**

" If the entire world decided to become vegan tomorrow, a whole host of the world's problems would disappear overnight. Climate change would decrease by 25 percent, deforestation would cease, rainforests would be preserved, our water- and air-quality would increase, life-expectancy rates would increase, and our rates of cancer would plummet, so certainly, with that one action of becoming vegan you are quite effectively making the world a better place. "

Source - Moby

Nuts About Truffles

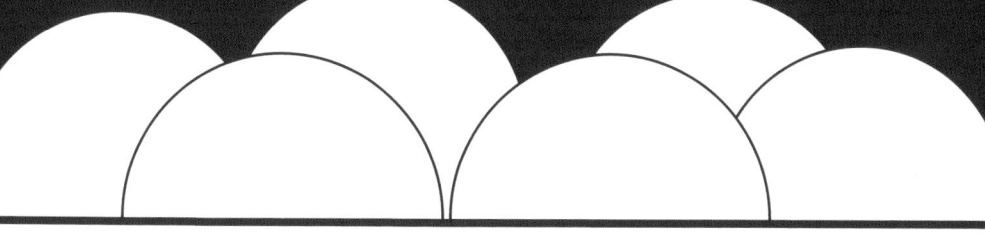

Coffee Truffles

Extra Chocolatey Truffles

Pistachio Coated Truffles

Flakey Truffles

Bounty Truffles

Salted Caramel Peanut Butter Truffles

Coffee Truffles

Serves: 15 - 20 | Total Time: 1 hour 45 minutes

Ingredients

The cream from a 400g can of coconut milk - see page V

280g of vegan chocolate

½ teaspoon of vanilla extract

2 teaspoons of decaffeinated instant coffee granules

Cocoa powder

Method

1. See page V

2. Put the **coconut cream** in a small saucepan and bring to boil using a low heat

3. Let it simmer for 5 minutes

4. Break the **chocolate** into pieces and set it aside

5. Add the **vanilla extract** and **coffee** to the **coconut cream**

6. Using the lowest heat setting, add a few pieces of **chocolate** to the pan containing coconut milk and stir the mixture

7. Keep stirring add adding more pieces of **chocolate** until it's all melted

8. Remove it from the heat and pour the contents of the pan into a container and set it aside to cool

9. After it's cooled, put it in the fridge for at least 1 hour

10. Use a spoon or ice-cream scoop to take some of the mixture and shape it by squeezing and rolling it into balls with your hands

11. Put them into a container and use a sieve to sprinkle **cocoa powder** on them (the more the better)

12. Put them in the fridge until you're ready to indulge!

Allergens: The chocolate may contain one or more of the major allergens.

Extra Chocolatey Truffles

Serves: 12 | Total Time: 45 minutes

Ingredients

200g of vegan dark chocolate	1 tablespoon of crushed roasted hazelnuts
7 tablespoons of vegan vanilla ice cream - I used Swedish Glace Smooth Vanilla Dairy-Free Ice Cream	30g of vegan hot chocolate powder

Method

1. Break the **chocolate** into small pieces and put them in a bowl
2. Heat some water in a pan and put the bowl of chocolate into the pan, keeping it there until the chocolate melts
3. While the chocolate is melting, take the **ice cream** out of the freezer so it warms up
4. Once the **chocolate** is melted, add the **ice cream** and the **crushed roasted hazelnuts**, 1 spoon at a time
5. Mix until it's smooth
6. Pour the mixture onto a plate lined with greaseproof paper
7. Let the mixture sit at room temperature for 30 minutes
8. Take small amounts of the mix and roll it into balls
9. Roll them in the **hot chocolate** powder and put them in a container

Storage: Keep them in an airtight container and they'll be good for a week.

Allergens: Nuts  **and Soya**

The hot chocolate powder or dark chocolate may contain one or more of the major allergens.

Pistachio Coated Truffles

Serves: 12 | Total Time: 45 minutes

Ingredients

200g of vegan dark chocolate	1 tablespoon of crushed roasted hazelnuts
7 tablespoons of vegan vanilla ice cream - I used Swedish Glace Smooth Vanilla Dairy-Free Ice Cream	A few tablespoons of ground pistachios

Method

1. Break the **dark chocolate** into small pieces and put them in a bowl
2. Heat some water in a pan and put the bowl of chocolate into the pan, keeping it there until the chocolate melts
3. While the chocolate is melting, take the **ice cream** out of the freezer so it warms up
4. Once the chocolate is melted, add the **ice cream** and **crushed roasted hazelnuts**, 1 spoon at a time
5. Mix until it's smooth
6. Pour the mixture onto a plate lined with greaseproof paper
7. Let the mixture sit at room temperature for 30 minutes
8. Take small amounts of the mix and roll it into balls
9. Roll them in the **ground pistachios** and put them in a container

Storage: Keep them in an airtight container and they'll be good for a week.

Allergens: Nuts and **Soya**

The chocolate may contain one or more of the major allergens.

Flakey Truffles

Serves: 12 | Total Time: 45 minutes

Ingredients

- 200g of vegan dark chocolate
- 7 tablespoons of vegan vanilla ice cream - I used Swedish Glace Smooth Vanilla Dairy-Free Ice Cream
- 1 tablespoon of crushed roasted hazelnuts
- 30g of grated vegan chocolate

Method

1. Break the **dark chocolate** into small pieces and put them in a bowl
2. Heat some water in a pan and put the bowl of chocolate into the pan, keeping it there until the chocolate melts
3. While the chocolate is melting, take the **ice cream** out of the freezer so it warms up
4. Once the chocolate is melted, add the **ice cream** and **crushed roasted hazelnuts,** 1 spoon at a time
5. Mix until it's smooth
6. Pour the mixture onto a plate lined with greaseproof paper
7. Let the mixture sit at room temperature for 30 minutes
8. Take small amounts of the mix and roll it into balls
9. Roll them in the **grated chocolate** and put them in a container

Storage: Keep them in an airtight container and they'll be good for a week.

Allergens: Nuts and **Soya**

The chocolate may contain one or more of the major allergens.

Bounty Truffles

Serves: 12 | Total Time: 45 minutes

Ingredients

200g of vegan dark chocolate

7 tablespoons of vegan vanilla ice cream - I used Swedish Glace Smooth Vanilla Dairy-Free Ice Cream

1 tablespoon of crushed roasted hazelnuts

2 tablespoons of desiccated coconut

Method

1. Break the **dark chocolate** into small pieces and put them in a bowl
2. Heat some water in a pan and put the bowl of chocolate into the pan, keeping it there until the chocolate melts
3. While the chocolate is melting, take the **ice cream** out of the freezer so it warms up
4. Once the chocolate is melted, add the **ice cream** and **crushed roasted hazelnuts**, 1 spoon at a time
5. Mix until it's smooth
6. Pour the mixture onto a plate lined with greaseproof paper
7. Let the mixture sit at room temperature for 30 minutes
8. Take small amounts of the mix and roll it into balls
9. Roll them in the **desiccated coconut** and put them in a container

Storage: Keep them in an airtight container and they'll be good for a week.

Allergens: Nuts and Soya
The chocolate may contain one or more of the major allergens.

Salted Caramel Peanut Butter Truffles

Serves: 16 | Total Time: 35 minutes

Ingredients

1 ½ cups of pitted dates (packed)	¼ cup of chunky salted peanut butter
2.5 tablespoons of melted coconut oil (divided)	1 cup of vegan dark chocolate chips (heaped)
¾ teaspoons of sea salt	

Method

1. Line a baking tray with greaseproof paper and set it aside
2. Blend the **dates** and 1 tablespoon of melted **coconut oil**
3. If it's not combining, add a teaspoon of warm water, scrape down sides and blend until a rough paste or ball forms
4. Add the **sea salt** and blend again
5. Use an ice-cream scoop or a tablespoon to create small balls of the mix
6. Put them on the baking tray mentioned in step 1 and put the tray in the freezer
7. Put the **peanut butter** and ½ a tablespoon of **coconut oil** in a bowl or pan and melt it in a microwave or on the cooker
8. Remove the truffles from the freezer and drizzle the peanut butter on them
9. Put them back in the freezer for 10 - 15 minutes
10. Put the **chocolate chips** and remaining tablespoon of **coconut oil** in a pan or bowl and melt it
11. Remove the truffles from the freezer and, use a fork to scoop them into the pan or bowl, so that they're coated in the melted chocolate
12. Wait for any excess to drip off, before putting them on the greaseproof paper again
13. Put them back in the freezer to set

Variations:
- Use reusable cupcake cases instead of a baking tray.
- For a different texture and look, try using smooth peanut butter.
- Sprinkle a small amount of sea salt on the truffles before freezing them for the final time.

Serving: Serve the truffles straight from the freezer, but if they've been in the freezer for over a day, take them out and let them to soften for ten minutes.

Storage: : They can be stored in the freezer for at least two weeks if not longer. Ours didn't last longer than that!

Tip: If you add too much water, they won't freeze well and they will be difficult to handle.

Allergens: Peanuts
The chocolate chips may contain one or more of the major allergens.

> It is far bigger than cutting down on your flights or buying an electric car, which would only reduce greenhouse gas emissions.
>
> Avoiding consumption of animal products delivers far better environmental benefits than trying to purchase sustainable meat and dairy.

Source - Joseph Poore quoted in The Independent

All Things Chocolate

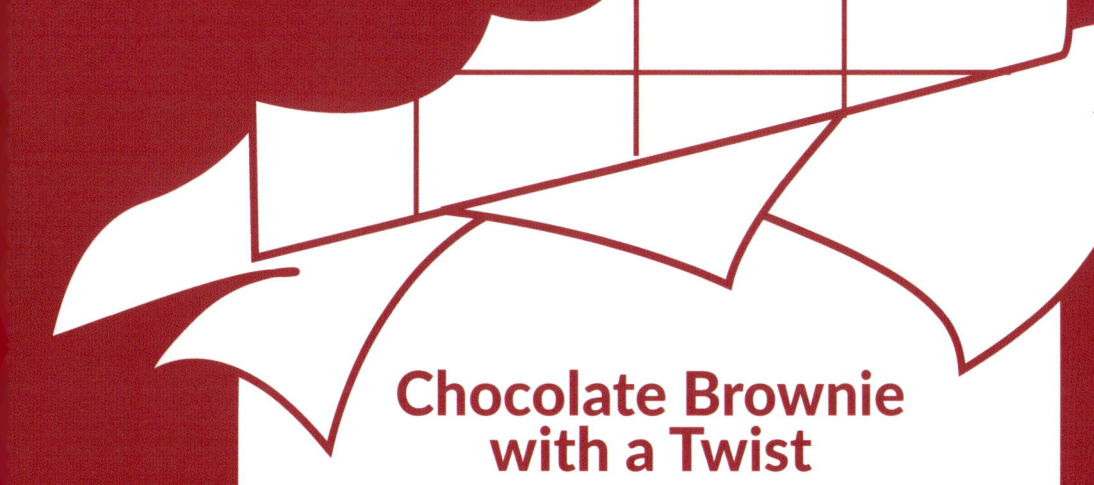

Chocolate Brownie with a Twist

Red Velvet Chocolate Chip Cupcakes

Chocolatey Cupcakes

Chocolate Coated Peanut Surprise

Choc and Nut Delight

Chocolate Cupcakes with a Surprise

Chocolate Brownie With A Twist

Serves: 4 | Total Time: 30 minutes

Ingredients

- ¾ tablespoon of ground flaxseed
- 1 ½ tablespoons of warm water
- 110g of dark chocolate
- ¼ cup of coconut oil
- 1 ½ tablespoons of cocoa powder
- ¼ cup of brown sugar
- ½ teaspoon of pure vanilla extract
- ½ cup of oat flour
- ¾ teaspoon of baking powder
- ¼ teaspoon of baking soda
- ¼ teaspoon of fine grain sea salt
- ½ cup of chopped pecan nuts
- ⅓ cup of dark chocolate chips
- 2 tablespoons of peanut butter
- Vegan ice-cream (you won't need the whole tub!)

Method

1. Put the **coconut oil** in a pan and warm it using a medium setting
2. Preheat the oven to 175 degrees Celsius
3. Mix the **flaxseed** and **warm water** and set it aside
4. Break the **chocolate** into pieces, put them in a bowl and add the **coconut oil**
5. Boil some water in a pan, and put the bowl containing the **chocolate** and **coconut oil**, into the pan
6. Stir the contents after 1 minute or so
7. Remove the bowl when the chocolate and coconut oil has melted and set it aside to cool
8. Mix together the **oat flour, baking powder, baking soda** and **salt**
9. When the **chocolate** has cooled, add the **flaxseed mix, sugar, cocoa** and **vanilla**, and mix it thoroughly
10. A little at a time, add the dry ingredients (see step 8) to the chocolate mixture, and stir until it's combined
11. Finally, add the **pecan nuts** and **chocolate chips** and fold them in
12. Use this to fill a quarter of each ramekin, gently pushing the mix so that the entire base is covered
13. Heat the **peanut butter** for a couple of minutes and add a layer of it to the ramekins
14. Add a similar amount of the chocolate mix to each ramekin
15. Put the ramekins in the oven for 20 minutes
16. Remove them from the oven and when you're ready to serve, heat them in a microwave until the dessert is a bit soft and warm and put a large scoop of **vegan ice cream** on top of the brownie and enjoy

Tip: The time needed to heat the brownie in the microwave can range from ten to forty seconds.

Allergens: Nuts and Peanuts

The ice cream, chocolate bar and chocolate chips may contain one or more of the major allergens.

Red Velvet Chocolate Chip Cupcakes

Serves: 16 | Total Time: 30 minutes

For Cupcake

Ingredients

- 2 cups of plain flour
- 1 ½ teaspoons of bicarbonate of soda
- 1 ½ teaspoons of baking powder
- 1 ½ cups of soft brown sugar
- ½ teaspoon of fine sea salt
- 1 tablespoon of cacao powder
- 1 cup of non-dairy milk - I used oat milk
- ½ cup of apple sauce
- 1 teaspoon of vanilla extract
- 2 tablespoons of oil e.g. rapeseed oil
- 1 ½ teaspoons of Dr. Oetker extra strong red food colouring gel
- 1 cup of dark chocolate chips

Method

1. Preheat the oven to 180 degrees
2. Put cupcake liners into a baking tray and set it aside
3. Put the dry ingredients in a large bowl and mix them together
4. Add the wet ingredients and mix it all together - I found it easier to use my hands
5. Keep folding the contents from the bottom of the bowl into the rest of the mix
6. Fill each case, ensuring it's no more than ¾ full
7. Bake for 25 to 30 minutes - check that the cupcake springs back when you touch it

For Frosting

Ingredients

- 170g of vegan cream cheese
- ¼ cup vegan butter - I used Pure Dairy Free Slightly Salted Butter Alternative
- 2 ½ cups of powdered brown sugar
- ¾ teaspoons of vanilla extract

Method

1. Use an electric whisk to beat the **cream cheese** and **butter** until it's fluffy
2. Add the **powdered sugar** and **vanilla extract** and using a low speed, mix it in with an electric whisk
3. Keep whisking until it's fluffy
4. Remove the cupcakes from the oven and let them cool before frosting them

Storage: Keep in an airtight container.

Allergens: Gluten

The chocolate chips and cream cheese may contain one or more of the major allergens.

Chocolatey Cupcakes

Serves: 16 | Total Time: 32 minutes

Ingredients

- 2 cups of plain flour
- 1 ½ teaspoons of bicarbonate of soda
- 1 ½ teaspoons of baking powder
- 1 ½ cups of brown sugar
- ½ teaspoon of fine sea salt
- 2 tablespoons of cacao powder
- 1 cup of non-dairy milk
- ½ cup of smooth apple sauce
- 1 teaspoon of vanilla extract
- 2 tablespoons of oil
- 110g of large vegan chocolate buttons

Method

1. Preheat the oven to 180 degrees
2. Put cupcake liners into a cupcake tray and set it aside
3. Mix all the dry ingredients in a large mixing bowl
4. Add the wet ingredients and mix all the contents together
5. Keep folding in the contents from the bottom of the bowl
6. Fill each case, making sure it includes one or two **buttons**
7. Stop filling them when the liner is ¾ full
8. Bake for 25 minutes and check that the cupcakes spring back when you touch them
9. Set aside to cool

Storage: Keep in an airtight container.

Allergens: Gluten

The chocolate buttons and the milk may contain one or more of the major allergens.

Chocolate Coated Peanut Surprise

Serves: 12 | Total Time: 60 minutes

Ingredients

¼ cup of crunchy peanut butter - I used the one by Meridian	5 shakes of salt
¼ cup of coconut cream - see page V	⅛ cup of quinoa
1 tablespoon of Golden Syrup	60g of dark vegan chocolate

Method

1. See page V
2. Put cupcake liners in a baking tray
3. Preheat the oven to 100 Celsius
4. Rinse the **quinoa** and spread it on a baking tray
5. Bake it for 15 minutes
6. Put the **peanut butter** and **coconut cream** in a bowl and mix it with an electric hand whisk until it combines
7. Add the **Golden Syrup** and **salt** and mix briefly
8. Remove the **quinoa** from the oven and toast it in a pan with a wide base so that you can spread it out and move it around while it's toasting
9. To avoid it burning, remove it from the heat when it has browned lightly
10. Add half of the peanut butter mix to the **quinoa** and stir
11. Create a layer of the peanut butter and quinoa mix in each cupcake liner
12. Put the other half of the peanut butter mix (which doesn't have any quinoa in it), on top of this
13. Put the cases in the freezer
14. Melt the **chocolate** in the microwave or by putting it in a bowl and placing the bowl in a pan of hot water
15. Remove the cases from the freezer and finish by adding the melted chocolate
16. Put them in an airtight container and keep them in the freezer for a minimum of 30 minutes or until you're ready to eat them

Allergens: Peanuts

The chocolate may contain one or more of the major allergens.

Choc And Nut Delight

Serves: 8 | Total Time: 30 minutes

Ingredients

1 cup of walnut halves	1 cup of natural peanut butter
1 cup of pecan halves	The cream from a 400g can of coconut milk - see page V
4 tablespoons of unsweetened cocoa powder	2 tablespoons of Maple Syrup
1 ½ cups of pitted dates	2 cups of vegan chocolate
1 pinch of salt	

Method

1. See page V
2. Heat some water in a pan
3. When the water is hot, put the **chocolate** in a bowl and place it in the pan so that it melts
4. While the **chocolate** is melting, blend the **peanut butter** and **maple syrup**
5. Add the **coconut cream** to the peanut butter mix, blend it and set it aside
6. Add half of the melted **chocolate** to the nutty base in the cake tin
7. Add the peanut butter mixture
8. Create a final layer with the rest of the melted **chocolate**
9. Put it in the fridge for at least 10 minutes before tucking in

Storage: Keep it in an airtight container in the fridge.

Allergens: Nuts and Peanuts
The chocolate may contain one or more of the major allergens.

Chocolatey Cupcakes With A Surprise

Serves: 16 | Total Time: 35 minutes

Ingredients

2 cups of plain flour	1 cup of non-dairy milk
1 ½ teaspoons of bicarbonate of soda	½ cup of smooth apple sauce
1 ½ teaspoons of baking powder	1 teaspoon of vanilla extract
1 ½ cups of brown sugar	2 tablespoons of oil e.g. rapeseed oil
½ teaspoon of fine sea salt	180g of dark chocolate
1 tablespoon of cacao powder	

Method

1. Preheat the oven to 180 degrees
2. Put cupcake liners into a baking tray
3. Excluding the **chocolate**, mix all the dry ingredients in a large mixing bowl
4. Add the wet ingredients and mix all the contents together - I found it easier to use my hands
5. Keep folding in the contents from the bottom of the bowl
6. Fill each case until it's a little over half full
7. Add 2 pieces of **chocolate** to each cupcake
8. Add more of the mixture but stop when the liner is ¾ full
9. Bake for 25 minutes and check that the cupcake springs back when you touch it
10. Remove them from the oven, let them cool and then pack them in an airtight container

Storage: Keep them in an airtight container.

Allergens: Gluten

The chocolate and the milk may contain one or more of the major allergens.

> "Becoming vegan is the most important and direct change we can immediately make to save the planet and its species."
>
> Source - Chris Hedges

Cheesecake Cheesecake And More Cheesecake

Gingerbread Cheesecake

Strawberry Cheesecake

Mini Chocolate Cheesecake

The Beauty of Biscoff

Gingerbread Cheesecake

Serves: 4 - 8 | Total Time: 3 hours 30 minutes

Ingredients

For the base

250g of McVities Ginger Nuts
5 McVities Hobnobs
3 tablespoons of vegan margarine
1 teaspoon of vanilla extract

For the filling

The cream from a 400g can of coconut milk - see page V
2 tablespoons of vegan icing sugar
340g of vegan cream cheese
2 tablespoons of caster sugar
½ teaspoon of vanilla extract (divided)
4 McVities Ginger Nuts biscuits
3 McVities Hobnobs

Method

1. See page V
2. Put the **coconut cream** into a bowl or jug that's deep enough for you to put an electrical hand mixer in
3. Add 1 teaspoon of the **vanilla extract** and all the **icing sugar** and blend it using an electric hand mixer
4. Put this in the fridge for at least 10 minutes
5. Blend 250g of **Ginger Nuts** and 5 **Hobnobs** until you have large crumbs and set aside
6. Melt the **margarine**, add it to the biscuits and mix it together
7. Put the biscuit mixture into the base of a cake tin and put it in the freezer
8. Blend 4 **Ginger Nuts** and 3 **Hobnobs** and set it aside
9. Using the same blender, (no need to wash it), mix the remaining **vanilla extract, cream cheese** and **caster sugar**
10. Remove the coconut cream mix from the fridge, add it to the items that are in the blender and mix it in using a spoon
11. Add the biscuit crumbs which were set aside in step 8
12. Remove the base of the cheesecake from the freezer and pour the creamy mix onto it
13. Use a spatula or spoon to make the top layer smooth and put it back in the freezer
14. Remove it from the freezer 2 hours before you want to serve it

Allergens: Gluten

The Cream cheese may contain one or more of the major allergens.

Strawberry Cheesecake

Serves: 4 - 8 | Total Time: 3 hours 25 minutes

Ingredients

- 220g of vegan digestive biscuits
- 10 McVities Hobnobs
- 6 tablespoons of vegan margarine
- The cream from a 400g can of coconut milk - see page V
- 2 tablespoons of vegan icing sugar
- 340g of vegan cream cheese
- 2 tablespoons of caster sugar
- 1 ½ teaspoons of vanilla extract (divided)
- 180g of fresh strawberries
- 3 large strawberries
- ½ tablespoon of Cornflour
- 1 tablespoon of water
- 2 tablespoons of Strawberry Jam

Method

1. See page V
2. Put the **coconut cream** into a bowl or jug that's deep enough for you to easily use an electric hand mixer
3. Add 1 teaspoon of **vanilla extract** and the **icing sugar** and blend it together
4. Put this in the fridge for at least 10 minutes
5. Blend the **biscuits** until you are left with crumbs
6. Melt the **margarine**, add it to the **biscuits** and mix it with a spoon
7. Pour this into a cake tin, flatten it to cover the entire base and put it in the freezer
8. Using the same blender, (no need to wash it), blend the remaining **vanilla extract, cream cheese** and **caster sugar** together
9. Remove the coconut cream mix from the fridge, add it to the blender and mix it with a spoon
10. Remove the cake tin from the freezer and pour the creamy mix onto the base
11. Use a spatula or spoon to make the top of the cheesecake smooth and put it back in the freezer
12. Remove the cheesecake 2 hours before serving
13. Before serving it, mash 180g of **strawberries** in a pan, add the **jam** and bring gently to boil
14. Add the **cornflour** to the **water** and mix
15. Add this cornflour mix to the pan and stir until it reduces and thickens
16. Let it cool and then pour it over the defrosted cheesecake
17. Slice the **large strawberries**, decorate the cheesecake with them and serve

Variations:
- Instead of making one big cheesecake, you could use ramekins to make individual portions.
- Instead of making a strawberry compote, heat 250g of strawberry jam with 4 tablespoons of water on a low setting, and after it cools pour it onto the cheesecake.

Allergens: Gluten
The cream cheese may contain one or more of the major allergens.

Mini Chocolate Cheesecakes

Serves: 4 - 8 | Total Time: 3 hours 25 minutes

Ingredients

110g of vegan digestive biscuits

5 McVities Hobnobs

3 tablespoons of vegan margarine

Half of the cream from a 400g can of coconut milk - see page V

1 tablespoon of vegan icing sugar

170g of vegan cream cheese

1 tablespoon of caster sugar

¾ teaspoon of vanilla extract (divided)

35g of chocolate

5 pistachios

Method

1. See page V

2. Put half of the **coconut cream** into a bowl or jug that's deep enough for you to use an electric hand mixer in

3. Add half a teaspoon of **vanilla extract** and the **icing sugar** to the coconut cream and blend it together using an electric hand mixer

4. Put this in the fridge for at least 10 minutes

5. Adding a few at a time, blend the **biscuits** until you are left with crumbs

6. Melt the **margarine**, add it to the **biscuits** and mix it together using a spoon

7. Get 4 cake tins out - they should have a diameter of about 5 inches

8. Pour the contents of the blender into the cake tins

9. Flatten the mixture and freeze them

10. Using the same blender, (no need to wash it), blend the remaining **vanilla extract**, **cream cheese** and **caster sugar** together

11. Removing the coconut cream mix from the fridge, add it to the blender and mix it with a spoon

12. Remove the cake tins from the freezer and pour the creamy mix onto the bases

13. Use something to make the top of the cheesecakes smooth and put them back in the freezer

14. Remove the cheesecakes 2 hours before serving

15. Just before serving, heat some water in a pan

16. When it's boiled, put the **chocolate** in a bowl and put the bowl in the hot water, so that the chocolate melts

17. Pour it over the cheesecakes

18. Chop the **pistachios** and use them to garnish the cheesecakes

Allergens: Nuts and **Gluten**

The chocolate and cream cheese may contain one or more of the major allergens.

The Beauty Of Biscoff

Serves: 4 - 8 | Total Time: 4 hours 30 minutes

Ingredients

75g of vegan margarine	340g of soft vegan cheese
20 McVities Hobnobs	15 Biscoff biscuits (divided)
200g of Biscoff spread (smooth or crunchy is fine)	

Method

1. Melt the **margarine** in a small pan
2. Crush 10 of the biscuits and mix them with the melted **margarine**
3. Press this down into a flan dish or a loose-bottomed cake tin
4. In a large bowl, mix all the **cheese** with the **Biscoff spread**
5. Spread this mixture carefully onto the biscuit base
6. Decorate it by pushing the remaining biscuits into the cake
7. It will set after being in the freezer for about 4 hours
8. When you're ready to eat it, keep it in a cool place for an hour before cutting it into slices

Variations:
When it's firm, garnish it using crumbs of Biscoff biscuits.

Allergens: Gluten and Soya
The cheese may contain one or more of the major allergens.

" Veganism is not about giving anything up or losing anything; it is about gaining the peace within yourself that comes from embracing nonviolence and refusing to participate in the exploitation of the vulnerable "

Source - The Independent

Family Creations

Sweet and Savoury Delight

Weetabix Paak

Sweet And Savoury Delight

Serves: 9 | Total Time: 30 minutes

Ingredients

2 ¼ cups of peanut butter	1 ⅓ cups of vegan dark chocolate
1 ½ teaspoons of coconut oil	½ cup of vegan milk
1 banana	

Method

1. Blend the **peanut butter** and **coconut oil** together
2. Press it into ramekins so that the bases are covered
3. Slice the **banana** and add a couple of pieces to each ramekin. Keep a few slices aside for step 11.
4. Put the ramekins in the freezer
5. Chop the **chocolate** into small pieces
6. Put the pieces of **chocolate** in a bowl and put the bowl in a pan of water
7. Melt the **chocolate** by boiling the water in the pan
8. After a couple of minutes, add the **milk** to the **chocolate** and stir
9. Make sure it's on a low heat and keep stirring until all the chocolate has melted
10. Remove the ramekins from the freezer and add a layer of the ganache
11. Garnish with slices of **banana** and store in the fridge until you're ready to enjoy them

Tip: If you find it tricky to pour the ganache, wait until it's cooled a little.

Allergens: Peanuts

The chocolate and the milk may contain one or more of the major allergens.

Weetabix Paak

Serves: 30 | Total Time: 1 hour 30 minutes

Ingredients

8 pieces of original size Weetabix	125g of ground Light Digestive biscuits
125g of Stork - the block that's sold in foil packaging is vegan	1 heaped teaspoon of ground cardamom
4 tablespoons of soya milk	½ teaspoon of ground nutmeg
240g of ground almonds	½ gram of saffron
125g of desiccated coconut	330g of condensed soya milk

Method

1. Decide how thick you want the Paak to be, and find a dish or tray that matches that
2. Then line it with greaseproof paper
3. Melt the **Stork** and set it aside
4. Heat the **soya milk** and when it's warm, add the **saffron**, give it a stir and set it aside
5. Put the **almonds, coconut, biscuits, ground cardamom** and **nutmeg** in a bowl and mix
6. Add the milk (step 4) to the items in step 5 and mix it quickly
7. Add all the remaining ingredients and mix again
8. Spread the mixture onto the greaseproof paper and pat it down so that it's even
9. Set it aside for 1 hour before cutting it into slices
10. Wait for 3 to 4 hours before removing it from the greaseproof paper

Allergens: **Nuts** **Gluten** and **Soya**

" All the livestock in the world cause more air pollution than all the cars, buses, planes, ships and other modes of transportation in the world combined. "

Source - Global Citizen

Gifts From Europe

Tiramisu

Meringue

Tiramisu

Serves: 8 | Total Time: 15 minutes

Ingredients

2 heaped teaspoons of instant coffee powder

½ mug of boiled water

300ml of soya cream

150g of vanilla desserts - Provamel Vanilla Soya Dessert and Alpro Vanilla Soya Dessert work well

18 McVities Rich Tea

Cocoa powder

Method

1. Use the **boiled water** and **instant coffee powder** to make a strong coffee in a bowl that's big enough to put the biscuits in and set it aside

2. Use an electric hand whisk to whip the **cream**

3. Add the **vanilla desserts** one at a time and mix it using the hand whisk

4. When the mixture is smooth and creamy put it in the fridge

5. Dip a **biscuit** into the **coffee**, wait until it has absorbed some of it and try and remove it before it breaks.

6. Put the **biscuit** at the bottom of a ramekin and repeat until there are 2 biscuits in each ramekin – they need to cover the entire surface, and it's fine for the biscuits to overlap

7. Add a layer of the creamy mix and use the back of a spoon or a spatula to spread it evenly across the ramekin

8. Finally, use a sieve to sprinkle a generous layer of **cocoa powder** over the top

9. Refrigerate for 1 - 2 hours before serving

Allergens: Gluten and Soya

Meringue

Serves: 12 | Total Time: 1 hour 30 minutes

Ingredients

- Aquafaba i.e. the brine from a 400g tin of chickpeas
- ¼ teaspoon of cream of tartar
- 225g of caster sugar
- 400ml coconut milk, well-shaken, then chilled in the fridge overnight
- 1 tablespoon of icing sugar
- 1½ teaspoons of vanilla extract
- 200g of strawberries

Method

1. See page V
2. Preheat the oven to 140°C (fan) or 120°C (gas mark 1)
3. Line a large baking tray with baking paper.
4. In a large bowl, whisk the **Aquafaba** and **cream of tartar** with an electric hand whisk until it forms stiff peaks
5. Once stiff, add the **caster sugar**, a spoonful at a time, and carry on whisking until it's glossy, firm and the contents don't move if you tip the bowl
6. Spoon the mix onto the baking paper and cook it in the oven for 1 hour.
7. Turn the oven off, leave the door ajar and let the meringues cool in the oven
8. Remove the solid parts from the can of **coconut milk** and put it in a bowl, along with the **icing sugar** and **vanilla extract**
9. Whisk it until soft peaks form and set aside
10. Slice the **strawberries**
11. Garnish your meringues with the **coconut cream** and **strawberries**

Storage: If you can resist, and if kept in an airtight container, the meringues will last for about five days.

> The findings reveal that meat and dairy production is responsible for 60 per cent of agriculture's greenhouse gas emissions, while the products themselves providing just 18 per cent of calories and 37 per cent of protein levels around the world.

Source - The Independent

In Ten Minutes Or Less

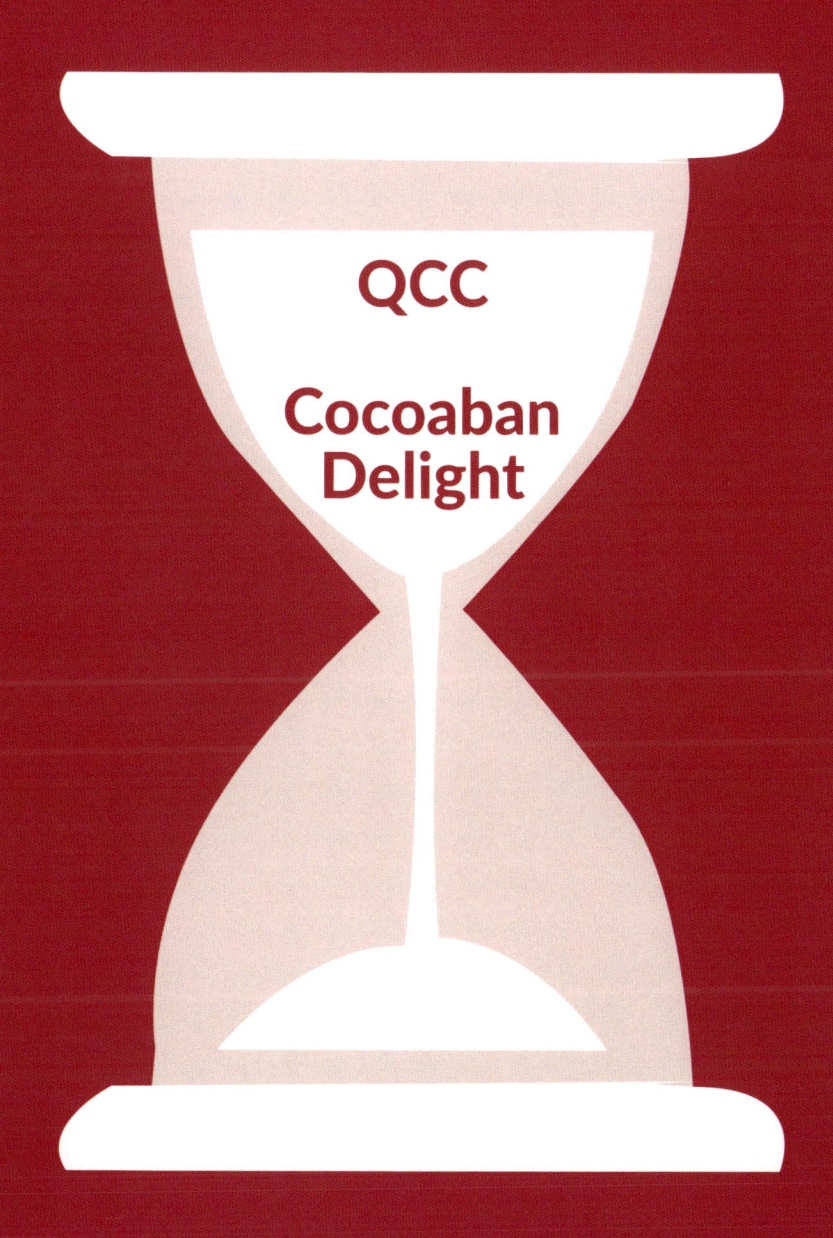

QCC

Cocoaban Delight

QCC [Quick Crispy & Cooling]

Serves: 1 | Total Time: 3 minutes

Ingredients

2 scoops of Swedish Glace Smooth Vanilla flavoured iced non dairy dessert	3 tablespoons of a sweet, crunchy vegan cereal - I used Sainsbury's Pecan and Maple Crisp

Method

1. Put 1 scoop of the **Swedish Glace** in a glass or bowl
2. Add the **cereal**
3. Add the remaining scoop of **Swedish Glace**
4. Enjoy :)

Allergens: Nuts Gluten and Soya

Cocoaban Delight

Serves: 4 | Total Time: 10 minutes

Ingredients

3 ripe bananas

The cream from a 400g can of coconut milk - see page V

2 tablespoons of hot chocolate powder - I like Twinings Swiss chocolate drink

3 tablespoons of smooth peanut butter - I use Peanut Butter by Meridian

Method

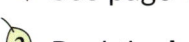

1. See page V
2. Peel the **bananas** and chop them into chunks
3. Put them in the freezer for 5 minutes
4. Blend the **coconut cream, hot chocolate powder** and **peanut butter** together
5. Add the chunks of **banana** and blend it again
6. Put this in 4 glasses or small bowls and enjoy

Allergens: Peanuts
The hot chocolate powder may contain one or more of the major allergens.

" It is far bigger than cutting down on your flights or buying an electric car, which would only reduce greenhouse gas emissions.

Avoiding consumption of animal products delivers far better environmental benefits than trying to purchase sustainable meat and dairy. "

Source - Joseph Poore quoted in The Independent

Recipe That Need Time To Chill Or Set

Chia Delight

Peanut Butter Cookies (Pg 7)

Halwa (Pg 17)

Gingerbread Cheesecake (Pg 53)

Strawberry Cheesecake (Pg 55)

Mini Chocolate Cheesecakes (Pg 57)

Beauty Of Biscoff (Pg 59)

Chia Delight

Serves: 2 | Total time: 9 hours

Ingredients

- ½ cup of Chia Seeds
- 1 cup of coconut milk
- ¼ cup of vegan coconut yoghurt
- 1 teaspoon of maple syrup (optional)
- 10 strawberries (divided)
- 1 tablespoon of Sainsbury's Pecan and Maple Crisp

Method

1. Put the **chia seeds** and **coconut milk** into an airtight container
2. Mix it together thoroughly, making sure that you reach the **seeds** at the edges and bottom of the container
3. Put the lid on the container and leave it in the fridge overnight
4. Check that the seeds have gelled, mix again and add the **coconut yoghurt**
5. If you are happy with the thickness and richness of the Chia Delight, leave it as it is, but if not, add more **yoghurt**
6. If you think it will be sweet enough once the fruit has been added, leave it as it is, but if not, add the **maple syrup** and mix it in
7. Blend 8 of the **strawberries**
8. Put some of the Chia Seed mix into 2 glasses or bowls
9. Add a layer of the blended **strawberries**
10. Repeat steps 8 and 9 until you've used all the ingredients up
11. Keep in the fridge
12. Depending on the look you are going for, roughly shop or finely slice the remaining **strawberries**
13. When you're ready to enjoy these desserts, garnish them with the **strawberries** mentioned above
14. Add some **Pecan and Maple Crisp** and you're ready to dive in!

Allergens: Nuts and Gluten
The coconut yoghurt may contain one or more of the major allergens.

About The Author

Heena Modi is a caring, compassionate and kind-hearted person who went dairy-free overnight after watching a video about the hidden realities of dairy production.

She didn't know anyone else who didn't consume dairy at the time, but that wasn't going to affect her, because she was clear about her reasons for going dairy-free. Heena did some research and soon learned about the cruelty involved in sourcing honey, eggs and other animal products, after which she shifted to a vegan diet.

She began looking for recipes, learning about alternatives to dairy products and found out which ingredients to watch out for when grocery shopping.
Heena learned about the harm involved in other things, such as clothing, accessories, shoes, cleaning products and cosmetics. She shifted to a vegan lifestyle and discovered how to find and buy these things without forfeiting style and choice.

It wasn't plain sailing all the way. Some of the obstacles she encountered included:
- Attending social events and feeling as if there was a big neon sign with the words "I'm vegan" over her head
- Struggling with how to explain why she shifted to a vegan lifestyle
- Feeling the need to convince others that veganism is not a hindrance to good health
- For Heena, vegan living has now become effortless and joyful

Heena created PlantShift.com to share information that would support informed decision making, help dispel myths, and make the shift smoother and easier.

She wants others to have an easier time when they go vegan, and she also wants to help them stay vegan. For this reason, she offers individual coaching for existing, new, and potential vegans. You can find out more about this on **PlantShift.com/coaching**

I would highly suggest anyone making the decision to lead a plant based lifestyle to get Heena on their side. You'll be grateful you did!
- *Surinder Walia, London, UK*

I had some health issues and I needed some help. I approached Heena Modi to help me to better myself health-wise. It's the biggest investment I've made for myself. I achieved my goal, which was to lose weight, not in a rushed way but a healthier way. I'm looking forward to 2021, with a new healthier me. I would highly recommend her.
- *Mina, London, UK*

Heena is one of the most passionate vegans I've met. Her enthusiasm for animals, delicious vegan food, and a compassionate lifestyle is contagious and inspiring.
- *Leo Babauta, San Francisco, USA*

Heena helped me transition from a junk food Vegan to more healthy whole foods Vegan.
- *Steve Robinson, London, UK*

Heena has had a positive effect on me and has provided me with incredible resources to educate myself and be committed to being vegan.
- *Eva Babauta, San Francisco, USA*

I have been a vegan for over 3 years but wanted to become healthier and have some quick recipes up my sleeve. Heena not only helped me with this but she supported me in many other ways too. Many of these things were ones that I had not even thought of.

Heena's kind, happy and encouraging manner meant I could be completely honest with her. She never made me feel bad for not completing goals but instead remotivated me.

Me and my husband have now adopted these strategies. They have become effortless and are now part of our lifestyle. We both see the benefits and improvements. I couldn't have done it without her.
- *Nilpa, London, UK*

Other Books By Heena Modi

The Way To A Vegan's Heart: Delicious Recipes To Help You Eat Well, Cook Quickly And Feel Content

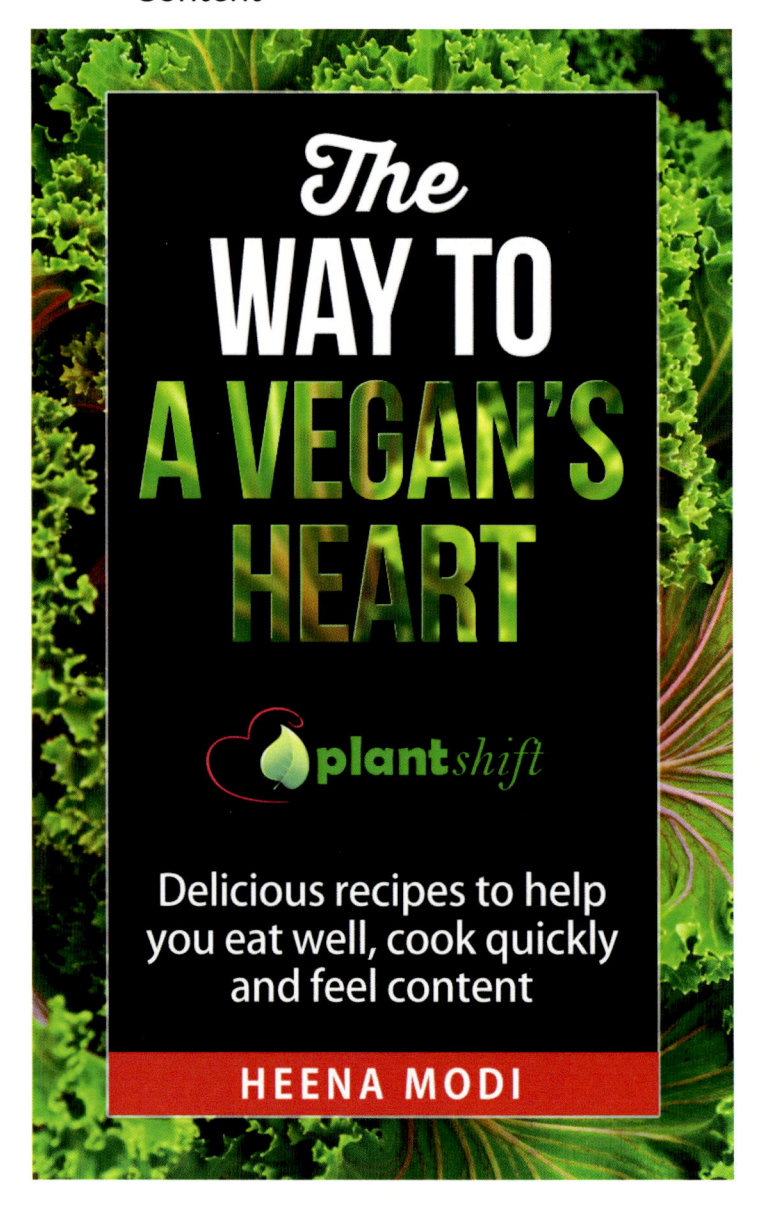

"This is a great addition to the library of vegan recipe books. Heena has put together a good range of mainly simple dishes which are rich in flavours and contain lots of twists on some old favourites. I'm looking forward to experimenting with them in the coming months!"

— Richard, who ran a vegan bed and breakfast in New Forest, with his wife Sandra, for 10 years

"For someone struggling with reconciling their ethics with their traditional dietary beliefs I found this book to be an inspiration. It's given me some great ideas for alternatives to my regular meals and as a personal trainer I will certainly be pointing my clients seeking a vegan shift towards this resource."

— Chris

"Simple and easy to follow yet highly interesting and delicious vegan recipes; neatly supplemented with a collection of feel-good quotes and common sense arguments for going vegan. Personal favourite would have to be the sweet and savoury banana!"

— Austin

"I have been waiting for a book like this for years. Thank you Heena!"

— Kev

"Fantastic book, easy to follow. Modern exciting recipes to inspire you and to help you with that dreaded question " What should we have for dinner?" The author comes across as thoughtful and makes the recipes easy to work with her main intention is to make being vegan EASY not a chore! A must read. I cant wait to try all the recipes out of this book! They all sound so delicious and nutritious!!"

— Shahnaz

"Yummy yummy yummy! Lovely selection of vegan dishes which are easy to prepare. The soup recipes look tasty and I am going to try the kale crisps this weekend. Nice and easy variety of recipes for vegans and meat eaters wanting to eat non-meat healthy meals."

— Ntathu

"Great ideas on how to create quick and healthy food. The book has plenty of new recipes that will excite your creativity!"

— D